A TRUE BOOK™

The Spanish Missions of New Mexico

ROBIN LYON

Children's Press®
An Imprint of Scholastic Inc.
New York Toronto London Auckland Sydney
Mexico City New Delhi Hong Kong
Danbury, Connecticut

Content Consultant
Donald E. Chipman
Emeritus Professor of History
University of North Texas
Denton, Texas

Library of Congress Cataloging-in-Publication Data

Lyon, Robin.
  Spanish missions of New Mexico / by Robin Lyon.
      p. cm.—(A true book)
  Includes bibliographical references and index.
  ISBN-13: 978-0-531-20579-2 (lib. bdg.)   978-0-531-21242-4 (pbk.)
  ISBN-10: 0-531-20579-7 (lib. bdg.)   0-531-21242-4 (pbk.)

  1. New Mexico—History—To 1848—Juvenile literature. 2. Missions,
Spanish—New Mexico—History—Juvenile literature. 3. Indians of North
America—Missions—New Mexico—Juvenile literature. 4.
Franciscans—Missions—New Mexico—History—Juvenile literature.
I. Title. II. Series.

  F799.L96 2010
  978.9'02—dc22   2009014705

All rights reserved. Published in 2010 by Children's Press, an imprint of Scholastic Inc.
Published simultaneously in Canada. Printed in China.
SCHOLASTIC, CHILDREN'S PRESS, A TRUE BOOK, and associated logos are trademarks and/or
registered trademarks of Scholastic Inc.

1 2 3 4 5 6 7 8 9 10 R 19 18 17 16 15 14 13 12 11 10   62

Find the Truth!

Everything you are about to read is true *except* for one of the sentences on this page.

Which one is **TRUE**?

T or F   Spanish explorers found a city of gold in New Mexico.

T or F   The Spanish introduced watermelons to Native Americans at the New Mexico missions.

Find the answers in this book.

Contents

THE BIG TRUTH!

Native Americans in New Mexico

Juan de Oñate

4

Spanish explorers introduced horses to what is today New Mexico.

Mission San Gregorio at Abó Pueblo

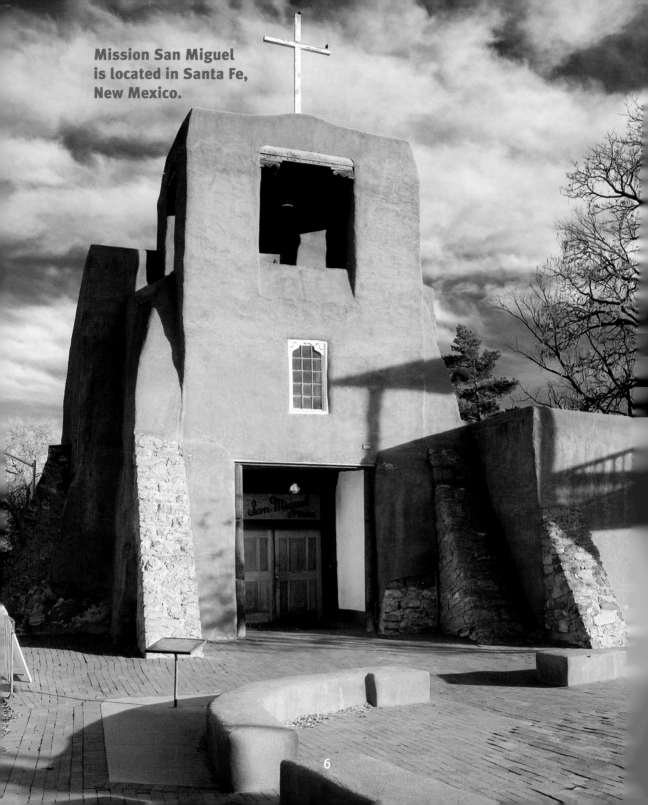

Mission San Miguel is located in Santa Fe, New Mexico.

CHAPTER 1

Into New Mexico

In 1598, Spanish priests set up the first mission in what is now New Mexico. At these missions, priests worked to **convert** Native Americans to Christianity. The missions were like villages where Native Americans learned European farming methods. By 1680, the Spanish had built dozens of missions in New Mexico. Mission San Miguel, the oldest mission still standing in New Mexico, was built in 1610.

The oldest church in the United States is at Mission San Miguel.

The Spanish Arrive

The Spanish first arrived in North America in 1492. In the early 1500s, they conquered what is now Mexico and were looking for more land to take over. In their search, the Spanish moved farther to the north and eventually arrived in what is now New Mexico. There they built missions to help establish their control over the region and convert Native people to Christianity.

A missionary preaches in New Mexico.

Tough Times

Arriving in New Mexico, **missionaries**, who had been sent by Spain, faced many difficulties. They were exploring unknown areas and adjusting to a hot, dry **climate**. When the missionaries met local Native Americans, there was often conflict. The Spanish forced their ideas on the Native Americans. Most Native Americans, however, did not want to give up their religious beliefs or their lifestyles.

CHAPTER 2

Exploring New Mexico

When the Spanish reached Mexico in 1519, they found gold and other riches. Before long, they hoped to discover a "new Mexico," where they could find even more wealth. In 1539, Catholic priest Marcos de Niza (MAR-kos DAY NEE-za) led an **expedition** from Mexico to today's New Mexico. He had heard tales of the Seven Cities of Cíbola (SEE-bo-luh), where the buildings were made of gold.

Native Americans helped the Spanish search for Cíbola.

Searching for Riches

De Niza traveled as far as what is today Zuni
(ZOO-nee), New Mexico, before returning to Mexico
with reports of fabulous riches in the north. In 1540,
explorer Francisco Vázquez de Coronado (fran-SEES-
koh VAS-kes DAY kor-oh-NAH-doh) headed north
to continue the search. For two years, Coronado
crisscrossed New Mexico and nearby areas before
returning to Mexico empty-handed. After this, the
Spanish lost interest in New Mexico for many years.

Coronado led more than 1,000 men on
his journey through the Southwest.

Cities of Gold

An old **legend** kept the Spanish interested in exploring New Mexico. It told of seven priests who had left Spain. They traveled far from Europe, to a land called Cíbola, and founded seven cities filled with gold. Many people searched for these cities, hoping to strike it rich. Father de Niza claimed he found one of the cities in New Mexico. When Coronado went searching in 1540, he discovered that the city didn't actually exist.

Spanish coins

13

Settling New Mexico

By 1598, Spain already ruled Mexico and Peru as well as other lands throughout the Caribbean Sea. The Spanish decided they should also conquer New

Mexico. Explorer Juan de Oñate (WAN DAY oh-NYAH-tay) was given the job of settling a **colony** in the area. On his long journey to New Mexico, Oñate brought a group that included more than 400 priests and families who were interested in settling in New Mexico, as well as 7,000 cattle.

Juan de Oñate

Oñate in New Mexico

Oñate's group of conquerors left Mexico in January 1598. By the following April, he **claimed** New Mexico for Spain. Oñate soon founded Mission San Gabriel, the first Spanish mission in New Mexico. He acted cruelly toward the Native Americans living in the area. Oñate demanded they give his people food and other supplies.

Founding Missions

About 10 Spanish missionaries traveled to New Mexico with Oñate. The missionaries went to convert the Native Americans to their religion. They spread out across New Mexico and founded missions in Native American towns. The Spanish took control of these towns, and with that the missions became the centers of religion and government in these areas.

The Spanish conquered Native American towns and forced their ways and beliefs on the Native peoples.

Pueblo people entered kivas by climbing down a ladder.

Many different Native American groups in the Southwest built kivas.

Long Traditions

The Native Americans living in New Mexico grew crops, hunted, and traded across the region. They had their own ways of life, their own languages, ideas, and religious beliefs. Some Native Americans in New Mexico believed that human souls arose from inside the earth. Because of this, they held religious ceremonies in underground rooms called kivas (KEE-vuz).

Native Americans in New Mexico

Many different Native American groups lived in New Mexico when Spanish missionaries first arrived. They included Pueblo (PWEB-low), Navajo (NAV-uh-ho), Apache (uh-PATCH-ee), and other peoples. Some groups lived in villages called pueblos. Others were nomadic, or moved regularly. Today, these groups continue to celebrate traditions from long ago.

The Navajo

The Navajo grew corn and beans and later raised sheep and goats in northern New Mexico. Today, they are the largest Native American group in North America.

The Apache

Many different Apache groups lived in New Mexico. They were nomadic and highly skilled with horses. One of their best-known leaders was Geronimo.

Geronimo

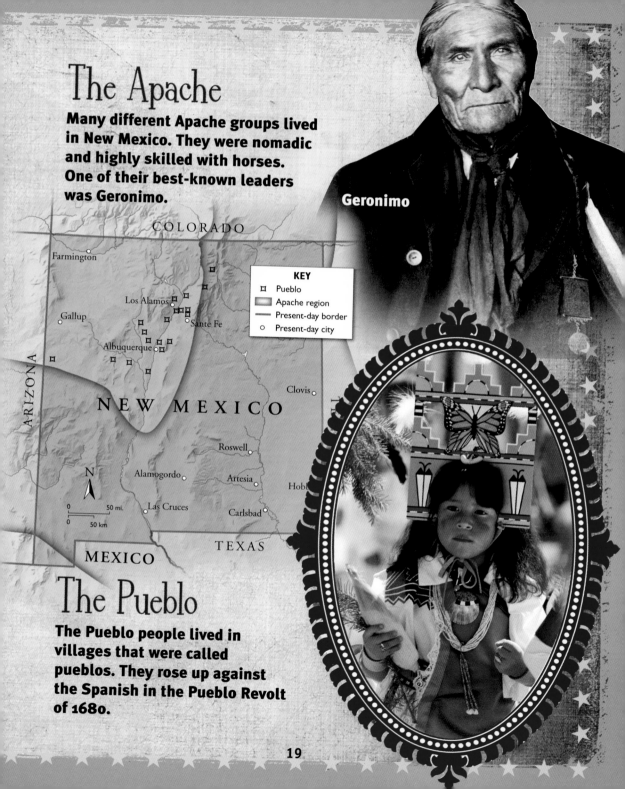

COLORADO

Farmington

KEY

▫ Pueblo
▢ Apache region
— Present-day border
○ Present-day city

Los Alamos

Gallup

Sante Fe

Albuquerque

ARIZONA

NEW MEXICO

Clovis

N

Roswell

Alamogordo

Artesia

Hobb

0   50 mi.

Las Cruces

Carlsbad

0   50 km

TEXAS

MEXICO

The Pueblo

The Pueblo people lived in villages that were called pueblos. They rose up against the Spanish in the Pueblo Revolt of 1680.

CHAPTER 3

Mission Life

Spanish missionaries set up missions to spread Christianity to Native Americans. Even if the Native Americans did not want to become Christian, the missionaries forced them to follow Christian religious practices. The missionaries also wanted to make the Indians loyal to Spain by teaching them the Spanish language and Spanish **culture**.

Native Americans and Spanish priests lived and worked at the missions.

The buildings at Zuni Pueblo were made of adobe bricks and stone.

Building the Missions

Many different buildings made up a Spanish mission. They included churches, schools, and homes. The Spanish and Native people constructed many of these buildings from **adobe** (uh-DOE-bee) bricks that could stand up to New Mexico's dry climate. Sometimes, the bricks were coated with plaster and painted white.

New Crops and Creatures

At the missions, Native people had many jobs, including making clothing and shoes. They were introduced to European ways of farming. The Spanish taught Native people to grow crops such as wheat and watermelons. The Spanish also brought horses, cattle, and sheep to the region. With horses, Native Americans were able to cover greater distances and hunt more easily.

Big Changes

The missionaries taught the Native Americans Spanish. This was sometimes helpful because Native people who spoke different languages could then communicate with each other in Spanish.

Many Pueblo people joined Christian events in their villages.

But many of the changes after the arrival of the Spanish were not good for the Native American people. The Spanish forced Native Americans to work for them and pay them taxes. Native people were expected to follow Spanish and Christian rules and traditions. Some Native Americans who broke the rules were beaten.

Native American Crafts

Many Native American groups in New Mexico are known for their beautiful crafts. Navajos weave rugs that feature stripe and diamond patterns. They use berries, leaves, and insects to dye the yarn rich colors. Navajos also make sand paintings, which are used as part of a healing ceremony. The Apache are known for their beautiful baskets, which are used to carry belongings. The Pueblo people make delicate pottery. Some also make kachina (kuh-CHEE-nuh) dolls, which represent spirits.

A Navajo girl weaves a blanket.

The original features of San Agustín have been preserved better than those of other missions in the region.

CHAPTER 4

Missions of New Mexico

One of the largest and oldest missions in New Mexico is San Agustín de la Isleta (SAN ah-goos-TEEN DAY LAH is-LAY-tuh). The mission was built in 1612 and is located south of the city of Albuquerque (AL-buh-kur-kee). It was constructed with adobe bricks, and its walls are 4 feet (1.2 meters) thick.

In Spanish, *isleta* means "little island."

Mission San Gregorio de Abó

The Tampiro (tam-PEER-oh) people founded Abó (ah-BO) Pueblo more than 400 years before Oñate passed through New Mexico. By the 1400s, the pueblo had become a center of trade. The Spanish established Mission San Gregorio at Abó Pueblo in 1622. The mission was abandoned by 1673 and fell into ruins. The ruins of Mission San Gregorio are now part of the Salinas Pueblo Missions National Monument.

Abó was one of the largest Pueblo villages.

The ruins of Mission San Gregorio de Abó include the remains of a round kiva.

The church at Mission Nuestra Señora de Purísima Concepción was about 40 ft. (12 m) high. That's twice as high as many mission churches in New Mexico.

Mission Nuestra Señora de Purísima Concepción

Mission Nuestra Señora de Purísima Concepción (NWES-truh see-NYOR-uh DAY poo-REES-ee-muh kun-sep-see-OHN) at Quarai (KWAR-eye) Pueblo, was built around 1628. Its church was made from red sandstone and built in the shape of a cross. Inside, the church had elegantly decorated **altars** (AWL-turz). The mission was abandoned in 1677 after **drought** (DROWT) and disease forced people from the area. Its ruins are part of the Salinas Pueblo Missions National Monument.

Pueblo people perform a rain dance in 1940.

CHAPTER 5

Growing Conflicts

As the number of missions grew across New Mexico, the Spanish often came into conflict with the Native Americans. The Pueblo people, especially, had become fed up with how the Spanish treated them. The Spanish would not allow the Pueblo to practice their religion and destroyed their holy kivas. In 1675, the Spanish arrested 47 Pueblo priests and punished them for not obeying Spanish rules.

Religious dances often expressed the Pueblo people's respect for nature.

Plan of Attack

A Pueblo religious leader named Popé (poe-PAY) organized most of New Mexico's Pueblo people and planned a **revolt** against the Spanish. They decided that, on a certain day, people in all of the Pueblo villages would destroy the local mission churches and kill the Spanish missionaries and settlers in the area. Afterward, the Pueblo rebels planned to join forces and attack New Mexico's Spanish capital, Santa Fe.

Popé means "ripe squash." ➜

Popé

The Pueblo Revolt

On the morning of August 10, 1680, the attacks began. Many mission priests and Spanish settlers were killed. Most of the missions were destroyed. By August 15, thousands of Pueblo rebels had gathered

Pueblo people from more than 24 villages took part in the revolt.

at Santa Fe and prepared to attack. The Spanish governor, Antonio de Otermín (an-TOE-nee-oh DAY oh-tayr-MEEN), decided to abandon the city and led nearly 1,000 Spanish settlers from the capital.

Escape to El Paso

The governor and settlers escaped to El Paso, in what is now Texas, where they spent the winter. Otermín planned to retake New Mexico, but his plans were not successful. Meanwhile, the Pueblo people worked to get rid of all signs of Christianity and Spanish influence in New Mexico. But some things introduced by the missionaries remained, including sheep, cattle, and fruit trees.

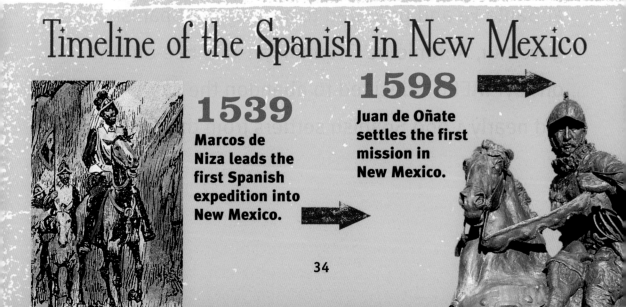

Timeline of the Spanish in New Mexico

1539
Marcos de Niza leads the first Spanish expedition into New Mexico.

1598
Juan de Oñate settles the first mission in New Mexico.

Return to New Mexico

In 1692, a small number of Spanish soldiers and priests led by a new governor, Diego de Vargas (dee-EH-go DAY VAR-gus), left El Paso to try to take back Santa Fe. The Pueblos surrendered to them. But when de Vargas returned to Santa Fe with the settlers who had fled, the Pueblos stopped them. After two weeks, the Spanish took over the city. They killed many Pueblo people and forced hundreds of others to work for them for the next 10 years.

1680
The Pueblo Revolt forces the Spanish out of New Mexico.

1692
The Spanish return to New Mexico.

35

Early Spanish flag

New Problems

After the Pueblo Revolt, the Spanish rebuilt some
of the missions that had been destroyed. This time,
they were more accepting of Pueblo culture. The
Spanish allowed the Pueblo people to speak their
own languages and practice their own religions. In
the 1700s, nomadic Native American groups often
attacked Spanish settlements and Pueblo towns.
The Spanish now needed the Pueblo people to help
them defend their settlements.

Pueblo people perform a religious ceremony called a corn dance.

Comanches fought the Spanish in the 1700s.

The Comanche first got horses in about 1680, and they quickly became skilled riders.

Comanche Clashes

Of these nomadic groups, the Comanche (kuh-MAN-chee) were the greatest threat to the Spanish. In the 1770s, the Spanish government set out to break the Comanche's power. During a battle in 1779, the Spanish killed Cuerno Verde (KWAER-noh VAYR-day), the Comanche's most powerful chief. The Spanish finally made a peace **treaty** with the Comanche in 1785.

Mission San Agustín de la Isleta's church rises above the other buildings in Pueblo Isleta.

CHAPTER 6

Times Change

By the 1800s, Spanish rule over New Mexico was coming to an end. At this time, the missions began to decline. Diseases brought by the Spanish killed many of the Native Americans, so the missions no longer had residents. As the Native Americans and the Spanish learned to live together, the missions became regular churches. They were no longer places where the Spanish could control the Native Americans.

Isleta was one of the largest New Mexico pueblos in the 1800s.

During the time of Spanish rule, the mission at Pecos was the largest European structure in North America.

Missions Today

Many missions still exist in New Mexico today. Some of them lie in ruins, while others have been preserved. Visitors to New Mexico can tour the Salinas Pueblo Missions National Monument, which includes ruins of mission churches from four different pueblos. These missions were all built between 1622 and 1660. Visitors can also go to Pecos National Historical Park, which contains the ruins of the pueblo of Pecos and two Spanish missions that stood there during the 1700s and 1800s.

The ruins of Abó mission are part of Salinas Pueblo Missions National Monument.

A ladder leads into a large kiva at Pecos National Historical Park.

San Esteban del Rey was one of the few missions to survive the Pueblo Revolt.

Still Active

Spanish missions had a lasting impact on New Mexico. The missionaries introduced horses, cows, and wheat to the area. Today, some of the original churches at the New Mexico missions are still used. Mission San Esteban del Rey (ES-tay-bahn DEL RAY) in Acoma was founded in 1629 and has been in use ever since. Mission San Miguel in Santa Fe is the oldest church in the United States. ★

True Statistics

Number of New Mexico missions: 33

First New Mexico mission: Mission San Gabriel, founded in 1598

Number of Pueblo villages before the Spanish arrived: 80

Number of Pueblo villages today: 21

Number of people Juan de Oñate brought to New Mexico: More than 400

Number of cattle Juan de Oñate brought to New Mexico: 7,000

Did you find the truth?

F Spanish explorers found a city of gold in New Mexico.

T The Spanish introduced watermelons to Native Americans at the New Mexico missions.

Resources

Books

Bial, Raymond. *Missions and Presidios.* New York: Children's Press, 2004.

Burgan, Michael. *New Mexico.* New York: Scholastic, 2008.

Ditchfield, Christin. *Spanish Missions.* New York: Children's Press, 2006.

Higgins, Nadia. *Spanish Missions of the Old West.* Vero Beach, FL: Rourke, 2007.

Stein, R. Conrad. *Spanish Missionaries: Bringing Spanish Culture to the Americas.* Chanhassen, MN: Child's World, 2005.

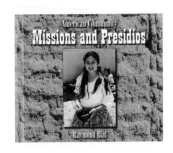

Organizations and Web Sites

National Museum of the American Indian

www.nmai.si.edu

See all kinds of Native American art and artifacts from the museum's exhibits.

New Mexico Tourism Department

www.newmexico.org/native_america/explore/index.php

Visit this site to learn about each of the missions settled in New Mexico.

Spanish Mission Churches of New Mexico

http://southwest.library.arizona.edu/spmc/

Discover a complete history of New Mexico missions at this site.

Places to Visit

Pecos National Historical Park

P.O. Box 418
Pecos, NM 87552
(505) 757-7200
www.nps.gov/peco/
This park contains the ruins of the Pecos Pueblo and mission.

Salinas Pueblo Missions National Monument

P.O. Box 517
Mountainair, NM 87036
(505) 847-2585
www.nps.gov/sapu/
Visit four sets of mission ruins at this national monument.

Important Words

adobe (uh-DOE-bee) – a building material made from sand, clay, water, and straw or manure and dried in the sun to make bricks

altars (AWL-turz) – raised platforms used for religious ceremonies

claimed – demanded as one's right

climate – the usual weather conditions in a place

colony – a place where a group of people live together under the control of their home country

convert – to cause to accept different beliefs

culture – the language, ideas, beliefs, and art of a particular group

drought (DROWT) – a long period of time with little or no rain

expedition – a journey taken for a specific purpose

legend – a story that has been made up and passed along

missionaries – people who are sent by a church or religious order to a foreign country to teach, convert, heal, or serve

nomadic – roaming from place to place

revolt – to rise up and fight against

treaty – an agreement

Index

Page numbers in **bold** indicate illustrations

About the Author

Robin Lyon writes fiction and nonfiction books for children. She also works as an editor and Web designer. She visited New Mexico as a child and saw Pueblo dances and adobe buildings.